Habits of the Wealthy

Adopting Behaviors That Drive Success

Table of Contents

Chapter 1. Introduction

Welcome to an exclusive voyage into the world of wealth and opulence, a Special Report that shines a light on the finely honed Habits of the Wealthy: Adopting Behaviors That Drive Success! Embark on this intriguing journey as we peel back the velvet curtain to reveal behaviors, strategies, and habits adopted by the financially successful. This Special Report isn't just a peek into their world, it's a step-by-step guide to cultivating the prosperous mindset they possess, encouraging you to build your own empire. Take the reigns, absorb the wisdom stored within these pages, and manifest your dreams into reality. Don't just aim to be wealthy; become it! Now is the perfect time to invest in your fortune by investing in this knowledge. Your golden future awaits!

Chapter 2. Unmasking the Mindset: Psychology of the Wealthy

Mastering the rules of the wealth game starts with understanding the mindset of its top players. This integral part of the journey to wealth unravels as a labyrinth of psychological traits and tendencies. The one thing that isn't as elusive, however, is the fact that anyone who aims to tread the path of prosperity needs to grasp this mindset first.

2.1. Grasping the Psychology of Risk

One of the key differences that separates the wealthy from others is their attitude towards risk. For most people, risk manifests as a force to be avoided. Yet, for the successful, risk is an ally. Embracing uncertainty, they harness its potential to yield unparalleled returns. They understand that risk and reward are two sides of the same coin. Investing in potentially high-growth businesses, starting a venture, or expanding into unfamiliar markets, the wealthy don't shy away from risk. Instead, they evaluate it. Each risky decision isn't just a gamble; it's a calculated move.

2.2. Persistence—The Silent Companion to Wealth

Wealth and success rarely come easy. They necessitate tenacity, resilience, and an unyielding resolve to keep striding forward even when the path gets rough. However, it's not about being stubborn or rigid in your approach. Rather, it's about learning from failures and devising more effective strategies. It's about having the courage to venture on, one step at a time, irrespective of the enormity or frequency of obstacles.

2.3. The Practice of Lifelong Learning

Embracing a lifelong commitment to learning is intrinsic to the psychology of wealth. Successful individuals are constantly challenging their knowledge base, seeking to expand it. Be it attending seminars, reading books, or learning from experienced individuals, they are active in seeking new information and insights. The pursuit of knowledge not only opens doors to innovative ideas but also prepares them to grab opportunities when they arise.

2.4. The Pursuit of Passion

The wealthy relish their journeys towards success, albeit riddled with challenges. Why? Because their motivation runs deeper than chasing money. There exists a profound passion for what they do. This passion fuels their energy and determination, driving them to push past their limits. Life becomes an exciting journey, and money merely a byproduct of their passion-fueled endeavors.

2.5. Building a Vision

Success is envisaged before it is realized. The same holds for wealth. High net-worth individuals don't just aim for monetary figures. They develop a comprehensive vision that encapsulates their goals, ambitions, and the life they aspire to lead. Building a vision encourages strategic planning and keeps them aligned with their ultimate goals.

2.6. Embracing Evolution

Indeed, the only constant in life is change. Wealthy individuals grasp this truth and adapt to evolving circumstances. They consistently analyze market trends, reassess their strategies, and fine-tune their approach to stay ahead of the curve. This adaptability ensures they are always in step with the changing tides of time.

2.7. The Power of Networking

Building wealth rarely happens in isolation. It's a collective effort, enhanced by a strong network of relationships. The wealthy understand this principle, hence actively build and maintain their networks. They nurture connections with likeminded individuals, collaborate with experts, and continuously expand their circle of influence.

2.8. Harnessing the Power of Time

Time is an extremely valuable resource, regarded as 'currency' by the wealthy. Instead of exchanging their time for money, they seek ways to make money work for them. This includes leveraging investment opportunities, passive income streams, and implementing time-saving strategies. Essentially, they focus on maximizing the return on their time investment (ROTI).

2.9. Curating a Positive Mindset

Last, but definitely not least, is the power of a positive mindset. Weaving a golden thread through all these behaviors, it is this positive and optimistic outlook that keeps wealthy individuals motivated. They choose to see challenges as opportunities, maintain an abundance mindset, and believe in their capabilities to achieve success.

Ingraining the mindset of the wealthy isn't a quick process, but rather the result of persistent efforts and conscious choices. By internalizing these traits and making them a part of your habitual behavior, you too can chart your path to wealth and success. Remember, the road to prosperity begins with the first step you take in your mind. It's time to take that step. Your journey begins now.

Chapter 3. Unearthed Scriptures: Learning from Billionaire Biographies

Delving into the chronicles of life stories of billionaires provides a wealth of knowledge, insights, and wisdom rarely gleaned from other sources. These narratives, a treasure trove of lessons, if studied in depth, could illuminate the path to success and accomplishment. We begin our journey by talking about the power of autobiographies, ways to interpret them, focusing on a select few impactful ones, and drawing valuable lessons from these narrations.

3.1. The Power of Autobiographies

Autobiographies wield enormous power to inspire, influence, and provide exclusive insights. They are a profound source of knowledge where individuals narrate their life courses, the highs and lows, challenges and triumphs, and the decision-making strategies adopted amidst life-altering circumstances. A billionaire's autobiography is particularly intriguing, as it uncovers the journey of an individual maneuvering through an exceptional path of creating significant wealth often from humble beginnings.

3.2. Mining Wisdom from Biographies

When reading the biographies of billionaires, don't just skim through the pages but mine them for wisdom, not just looking for what they did, but rather how they thought, decided, and resolved matters. Consider the context and relative impacts of each decision, observing the strategic thinking and action-taking behind them. A deep understanding of these factors assists in devising our own road maps to success.

3.3. Unforgettable Narratives: Noteworthy Billionaire Biographies

Several notable billionaire biographies offer fascinating revelations of their journeys. Here are three impactful narratives that we would be delving deeper into:

- 'Snowball. Warren Buffett and the Business of Life' by Alice Schroeder
- 'The Art of the Deal' by Donald Trump
- 'Losing My Virginity: How I Survived, Had Fun, and Made a Fortune Doing Business My Way' by Richard Branson

3.4. 'Snowball. Warren Buffett and the Business of Life'

Warren Buffet, the "Oracle of Omaha", is unarguably one of the most successful investors in history, as reflected in his biography. His investment strategies, principles, work ethics, and frugality despite immense wealth are heartening revelations. Diving deeper into Buffet's beginning as he ventured into life, his simple upbringing, and the humble life he retains despite tremendous wealth, underscores the power of integrity, and humility in leaders.

3.5. 'The Art of the Deal'

Donald Trump's 'The Art of the Deal' takes the reader through his early life, showcasing a determined and fearless character. We see a young man overcoming multiple adversities, risking large investments, and overcoming bankruptcies. This biography underscores the importance of perseverance, audacity, and resilience in the face of challenges in the journey to wealth creation.

3.6. 'Losing My Virginity: How I Survived, Had Fun, and Made a Fortune Doing Business My Way'

Richard Branson's biography adds a different flavor to the mix – it's not just about success and wealth but an adventurous ride reflecting Branson's innovative and original strategies. He reinvented the rules of business and is known for his rebellious nature, which established the Virgin brand as distinctive. The joy he finds in taking risks and keeping his fingers in many pies provides significant insights into the minds of serial entrepreneurs.

3.7. Lessons Drawn from Billionaire Biographies

The underlying patterns seen in these biographies reveal important lessons:

- Perseverance and Resilience: The path to wealth is filled with failures and setbacks. The capacity to stay the course and maintain faith in your vision is crucial.

- Integrity and Humility: Having strong moral principles and remaining modest despite vast wealth exemplifies extraordinary leadership.

- Audacity: Having the audacity to take risks, make large gambles, and endure losses could be the game-changer in amassing extraordinary wealth.

- Joy in Diversity: Finding thrill in engaging in diverse domains, not for the sole purpose of wealth, but for the joy of exploring novel ventures is an exciting entrepreneurial perspective.

In the end, it's not just about the story. It's also about the mindset, the strategies, and the attitude encompassing these narratives, which form the roadmap to success. These lessons unearthed from the scriptures of billionaires' lives can serve as guiding lights in your journey towards creating wealth and success.

Chapter 4. Mastering Money: Management Strategies of the Affluent

Understanding the essence of money management begins with one guiding principle: money is a tool, not an end. The affluent understand this better than most. They are not simply focused on accumulation but on effective utilization. Let's delve into their strategic methods, from budgeting to investing, and contemplate how we can imitate their wise patterns.

4.1. Embracing a Budget Oriented Mindset

Budgeting is to wealth what foundations are to a skyscraper. It may not be the most glitzy aspect of finance, but it is undeniably impactful. The wealthy understand the importance of having a robust budget that outlines their income and expenses, enabling them to retain control over their accounts and ensuring that they live within their means.

The general rule of thumb used by many successful individuals is the 50/30/20 rule for budgeting. Fifty percent of their income goes towards necessities, thirty percent towards their desires, and the remaining twenty percent goes directly into savings. However, personal finance is highly individualistic, and each individual may have a customized version of this model to suit their unique situation.

4.2. Investing With Purpose

Money left idle is money wasted. The wealthy understand this and make their money work for them. Investing is a common and effective method used by the affluent to grow their wealth. They are not risk-averse; instead, they understand that higher risks often come with higher yield. That said, they are also well aware that an unmitigated risk might lead to unwarranted loss.

Thus, they follow a planned investment approach, often utilizing a blend of low, medium, and high risk investments. The idea is to balance the risk/reward scenario and ensure that even if one investment falters, others can pick up the slack. Their investment portfolio often includes real estate, bonds, stocks, startups, and more. They also appreciate the power of compound interest and long-term growth.

4.3. The Power of Diversification

The adage 'don't put all your eggs in one basket' is a financial mantra for the wealthy. They invest in various fields, spreading their vulnerabilities and boosting their income potential. Diversification isn't just about spreading risk; it's also about increasing chances of returns. Exploring diverse sectors opens up multiple streams of income, building a safety net around their wealth.

4.4. Building an Emergency Fund

Nothing in life is certain, and economic downturns or personal emergencies can strike at any time. The wealthy protect their financial stability with a well-stocked emergency fund, designed to cover their expenses for at least six months. This practice offers a safety net against unforeseen circumstances, rendering them less reliant on credit, and more able to bounce back after a crisis.

4.5. Understanding Debt Management

Debt is not always detrimental. The wealthy often leverage debt to grow their fortune. Mortgages for real estate, loans for business ventures, even credit cards—all these can be valuable financial tools when used strategically and paid promptly.

For the affluent, debt becomes a tool, not a noose. It allows them to take advantage of opportunities they might not otherwise afford. However, they also know the importance of managing this debt effectively to prevent financial turmoil.

4.6. Leaving a Legacy: Estate Planning

For many wealthy individuals, estate planning isn't just about protecting their wealth; it's about leaving a legacy. They employ tax strategies, legal instruments such as trusts and wills, and succession planning to ensure their wealth does not diminish over generations, but thrives.

These are the key elements that construct the money management strategies of the affluent. They represent an adaptable blueprint for anyone determined to amplify their wealth. Remember, accumulating money is only the first half of the equation—the second half involves managing it astutely, growing it wisely, and preserving it for posterity.

Chapter 5. Visioneering Wealth: The Significance of Goal Setting

To set the stage for wealth creation, one must first understand a key component central to all success stories: goal-setting. Goals are the measure of progress, the destination to a journey, the blueprint for emerging successful pursuits. It is, perhaps, the single most profound similarity found among affluent individuals all over the globe, from self-made millionaires to billionaires who dominate the Forbes list. But, goal-setting in itself isn't merely about personal aspirations. Instead, it is a methodical and strategic approach towards achieving desired outcomes that unleashes the potential for wealth creation.

5.1. The Psychology of Goals

Goal setting is steeped in psychology, brewing a potent concoction of motivation, self-confidence, attention focus and reinforcement of behavior. For the affluent, it acts as a compass, delineating direction towards the desired destination of prosperity. How does this work? The psychology of goal-setting operates on the principles of intention, energy and focus.

Every goal begins with intention, a direction in which one wishes to steer their actions. This intention then precipitates energy, a certain momentum that sets the wheel of actions into motion. Lastly, the focus comes into play, narrowing down actions to those aligned with the intention alone, thus increasing efficiency.

However, merely understanding the psychology does not equate to goal mastery. Implementation of goal-setting requires strategic planning and unwavering commitment.

5.2. From Dreams to Reality: SMART Goals

Any successful journey begins with a well-charted map, and wealth creation is no outlier. The route to riches is best navigated through SMART goals. This ubiquitous acronym, standing for Specific, Measurable, Achievable, Relevant and Time-bound, is a blueprint for strategic goal planning.

Specific goals give clarity, eliminating vagueness and aiding the visualization process. Measurable attributes allow for tangible tracking of development, inspiring motivation and revealing areas needing improvement. Achievable ensures the objective is within the realms of reality, granting self-confidence. Relevance prioritizes goals having a direct relation to the overall aspiration of wealth building. Lastly, Time-bound brings a sense of urgency, nudging one into action sooner rather than later.

5.3. Leveraging Vision Boards

Visualization is a powerful tool wielded by the affluent. It's the act of manifesting future aspirations in the present, solidifying intent and bolstering motivation. Vision boards are a fantastic way to bring this method to life.

Exploring the benefits, vision boards make abstract goals concrete, they present a visual representation of the desired future, acting as daily motivation. Moreover, they act as a continual reminder of one's aspirations, reinforcing determination to stay on track.

5.4. Overcoming Potential Roadblocks

Wealth creation is not a straight highway but a terrain teeming with potential roadblocks. Financial barriers, distractions, and self-doubt are common obstacles. However, roadblocks lose their potency with well-prepared strategies.

Firstly, financial hurdles may be mitigated by critical analysis of one's current financial situation, debt management and setting up emergency funds. Equally important is the absorption of financial literacy to successfully navigate through future economic uncertainties.

Distractions get in the way when clarity of the objective fades. Here, affirmations, regular self-review of goals and the constant update of the vision board can be instrumental.

Self-doubt, the most menacing of all roadblocks, often leads to abandoning the wealth creation journey entirely. Counteracting self-doubt requires mental fortitude, resilient optimism and reinforcement from success stories and mentors.

Goal setting is far more than an initial step in the wealth creation process. It is, instead, a continually evolving strategy, a moral boost and a direct line to success. Regardless of the seeming enormity of the wealth goal, keep in mind that every wealthy individual began their journey with one simple, profound step: setting a goal. Once you master this step, you're already on your way to a golden future.

Remember, the journey to wealth isn't about a quantum leap;It's about numerous tiny steps leading you to a treasure trove of opulence. Start small, think big. The world of wealth is not as complex when navigated with clear, confident, and consistent goals. Begin today; Your golden future awaits!

Chapter 6. The Power of Persuasion: Maximizing Negotiation Skills

The art of negotiation and persuasion transcends just the boardrooms and business scenarios. It infiltrates our everyday lives, veiled in myriad forms - from bargaining at a local market to building our personal relationships. One could even argue that negotiation is an elemental part of human interactions. Women and men of wealth and success have, over the years, mastered this powerful tool and, by subtly swaying others' hopes and fears, they not only close impressive deals but also form valuable partnerships and alliances.

6.1. The Landscape of Negotiation

In the vast cornucopia of abilities that the wealthy and successful have, negotiation - the capability to convince others and make them see your perspective while ensuring a win-win outcome, is a particularly significant one. It is a common fallacy that negotiations are solely the realm of heavyweight corporates or businesspeople. However, in reality, every single human interaction can potentially be a negotiation.

Negotiating power does not just manifest in formal situations. Acquiring this skill can have phenomenal impacts on personal life, relationships, and self-development. Embracing the art of negotiation leads to more fulfilling interactions, greater control of our own narrative, and an enhanced understanding of the dynamics that govern various aspects of our world.

In essence, negotiation skills form a critical component of the arsenal adopted by the financially successful. The processes and mechanisms are applicable universally, regardless of the context. Successful negotiators are scholars of human behavior and demonstrate an innate knack for discovering and understanding the sources of resistance, their intentions, desires, fears, and motivations.

6.2. The Core Elements of Negotiation

Negotiation is not entropy, full of randomness and chaos. It follows certain fundamental principles:

1. Preparation: A well-prepared negotiator is like a scout with a map and compass. Preparation involves doing background research on your negotiation partner, understanding the context, identifying your objectives, and being aware of possible outcomes.

2. Communication: The bedrock of effective negotiation. It not just about eloquent talking; it's about active listening too. Understanding and acknowledging the other party's standpoint can go a long way in the negotiation process.

3. Win-Win Orientation: A successful negotiation should culminate in an agreement beneficial to all parties involved. The aim is to collaborate and create value rather than a binary win-lose outcome.

Practice these principles and see how they transform the results, driving you towards success. Remember, negotiation is not a battle but a skilled crafting of agreement, favoring all parties involved.

6.3. Decoding the Negotiation Strategies of the Wealthy

The financially successful have honed the art of negotiation through years of practice and experience. Hereon, we delve into the specific strategies they leverage to gain a competitive upper hand.

1. Research and Prepare: The wealthy understand that knowledge is power. So, they make an effort to gather as much information about the other party and the situation at hand before stepping foot into any negotiation.

2. Understand the Interests of the Other Party: They realize that every negotiation is about satisfying the interests of both parties. They spend considerable time understanding the needs, fears, and desires of their negotiation partners.

3. While they're assertive in their pursuit of their objectives, wealthy individuals also exhibit flexibility. While they keep their main objectives in sight, they exhibit a willingness to expand the scope of the negotiation, to accommodate concerns that vie for attention.

These strategies provide guidance into how the wealthy and successful dive into the art of negotiation, and offer valuable insights you can incorporate as you journey towards financial success.

6.4. Roadmap to Becoming a Skilled Negotiator

To instill these skills and become a proficient negotiator requires time, practice, and a bit of introspection. Begin by asking questions - lots of them! This not only makes the other party feel valued, but it also aids in revealing their underlying interests. It helps you "map the terrain" before you even begin to negotiate.

Another pivotal habit is cultivating patience. Negotiations can often take longer than anticipated, and rushing the process might not yield the desired outcome. At such times, it's important to keep calm and not let impatience get the best of you.

Lastly, become a keen observer. Pay attention to the subtleties of communication - both non-verbal and verbal. The tiniest of cues can reveal a wealth of information about the other party's psyche, thus giving you an upper hand.

To conclude, it is within everyone's grasp to master the art of negotiation. This powerful tool, so commonly observed among the financially successful, offers tangible steps towards cultivating a prosperous mindset. It's your turn now to adopt these habits, hone your skills, and create your own nexus of wealth and success.

Chapter 7. Health is Wealth: Focus on Fitness and Well-being

Every journey of wealth creation begins with an emphasis on the most precious resource: health. The connection between health and wealth is far from superficial. Being physically fit and mentally calm enhances focus, fuels drive, and cultivates the discipline required for wealth accumulation and preservation.

7.1. Understanding the Wealth-Health Connection

The relationship between wealth and health is symbiotic—each feeds into and enhances the other. As such, it is crucial to understand this connection if one wants to attain significant wealth.

Firstly, maintaining good health can drastically cut down on medical bills, both in the short and long term. The saying, "An ounce of prevention is worth a pound of cure," rings especially true in this situation. By maintaining a healthy lifestyle, you can reduce the risk of developing chronic conditions that drain bank accounts.

Moreover, physical health is directly linked to mental clarity, a vital component for making sound financial decisions. A healthy body contributes to better sleep and more energy, things that improve your overall cognitive function. With a sharper mind, one can make better investment decisions, create innovative ideas, and respond quickly and appropriately to changing financial situations or opportunities that arise.

Lastly, persistence, consistency, and discipline are traits that are common among the wealthy, and these are traits that are also developed through the journey of maintaining physical fitness and overall well-being. The dedication required to maintain a routine, the resilience to recover from setbacks, and the discipline to resist detrimental temptations are as essential in fitness as they are in wealth accumulation.

7.2. Incorporating Regular Exercise

Edmund Hillary, the first man to reach the top of Mount Everest, said, "It is not the mountains we conquer, but ourselves." Exercise is not merely a means to sculpt a healthy physique, but a mechanism through which we can also mold a resilient mindset—an aspect that is paramount in handling the ups and downs of wealth creation.

Developing and maintaining a regular exercise schedule increases physical stamina, reduces stress, and improves cognitive function. The physical effort that exercise demands is reimbursed through increased energy levels, better mood, and sharper focus—equipping you with the necessary elements to make astute financial decisions.

Moreover, exercise works as a prompt to eat healthily—another integral part of maintaining physical well-being. This dual focus on exercise and nutrition will aid in producing a ripple effect, benefitting all parts of life, including financial success.

7.3. Nutrition and Wealth: The Understated Connection

In essence, your body is a vessel, and its condition can impact all aspects of your life, including wealth acquisition. Nutrition, particularly, plays a much more significant role than many realize on the journey to wealth. A nutritional, balanced diet not only enhances physical health but also improves mental faculties—both requisite elements for the path to prosperity.

A diet packed with the necessary nutrients strengthens your physical capabilities, wards off diseases, and helps in maintaining a healthy weight—an important aspect of avoiding chronic conditions like diabetes and heart disease, which can impair both your health and wealth.

From a mental standpoint, nutrition is pivotal. For instance, Omega-3 fatty acids—found in fatty fish and nuts—contribute to brain health, aiding memory and mental performance. Foods high in antioxidants, such as leafy green vegetables and berries, can assist in combating stress—an unavoidable part of the wealth acquisition journey. Maintaining stable blood sugar, achieved through a balanced diet, plays a substantial role in defusing mood swings and nurturing steady focus.

7.4. Stress Management Techniques

While stress is an inevitable accompaniment on the road to riches, it is possible, and necessary, to cultivate techniques to handle this intrusive guest adeptly. High-stress levels can lead to physical and mental health issues that can sideline your ambitions and derail your journey to wealth.

Methods of dealing with stress vary widely, enabling you to select one that aligns with your preferences. Techniques range from meditation, a practice that calms the mind and redirects focus from external stressors to inner peace, to hobbies such as painting, reading, dancing, or gardening—any activity that brings you joy and diverts your attention from anxiety.

Physical competence and mental tenacity are both integral to wealth accumulation and preservation, and both are enhanced by maintaining good health. Wealth, like health, is not a destination but a journey, and taking care of the vessel that undertakes this journey -

your body - is the first and most vital step. Concentrating on fitness and well-being isn't simply a suggestion on the path of wealth creation; it is a prerequisite.

7.5. Bridging Wealth with Well-being

The relationship between wealth and health is intertwined such that ignoring health could soil your wealth creation plans. Physical fitness, nutrition, and mental well-being shape the resilience and intellectual faculties necessary for wealth accumulation.

As you embrace this understanding fully, remember that the real wealth is not just prosperity but a prosperous life as a whole. Thus, a truly wealthy person is not one who has stacks of money, but one who possesses health, peace, and financial stability in abundance. This perspective will help you balance the pursuit of wealth with the enjoyment of life's other riches, leading to a holistic version of wealth that includes comfort, contentment, and an overall feeling of abundance.

Thus, the wealth-creation journey begins by prioritizing health. Good health is, indeed, your most precious asset. Hence, as we start this captivating expedition into the world of wealth, it is best to begin by focusing on maintaining a rigorous fitness routine and encouraging overall well-being. After all, health is not just wealth – it forms the basis of all wealth! So aim for these fundamental aspects of life first and watch as your prospects of achieving financial success increase exponentially.

Chapter 8. Networking Nuggets: Building Strong Connections

In the prosperous world, your network is your net worth. Cultivating strong, meaningful relationships is a powerful technique utilized by those who thrive in an environment of opulence. Networking isn't merely about recognizing faces; it's about knowing the value each person brings to the table and understanding how synergies can benefit everyone involved. Here, we explore the keys to building and maintaining a wealth-driven network.

8.1. The Art of First Impressions

There's only one chance to make a first impression, and wealthy individuals know the value of making it count. This isn't about painting a false picture, but about presenting your best self—positive, ambitious, and open to possibilities. The best way to impress is to be genuine, as anything less can tarnish your reputation and weaken potential partnerships.

To be memorable, learn to listen more than you speak. In conversations, focus on the other person, showcasing your interest in them and their work. Utilize appreciative enquiry, listening attentively, absorbing, and asking insightful questions. Be assertive, but not aggressive. Confidence is attractive, but arrogance can be off-putting.

8.2. Cultivating a Personal Brand

In a world of intense competition, successful individuals work on creating a personal brand. This goes beyond job titles and degrees;

it's about your unique attributes, styles, values, and the methods by which you translate these into tangible business outcomes. Let people recognize you for your strengths and know that they can count on you for specific subject matters.

Just like businesses cultivate their brands diligently over time, personal branding is nurtured and built with patience and consistency. Align your actions, conversations, and social media presence with your intended brand. Evidence of inconsistencies can cast a doubt on your credibility, a risk that the wealthy are careful to mitigate.

8.3. Engaging in Active Listening

Wealthy individuals understand the power of being present in their interactions. They are active listeners, subtly signaling their interest and encouraging healthy dialogue. Rather than just waiting for their turn to speak, they have mastered the art of listening to comprehend, analyze and respond.

Effective active listening promotes mutual respect and understanding, paving the way for strengthened professional and personal relationships. Reacting appropriately to what is being said also earns the trust of your counterparts, which is particularly vital in business settings.

8.4. Building Long Term Relationships

Those seated on the pinnacle of wealth understand that true networking does not revolve around short-term gains. They aren't interested in what they can get from someone in the immediate future, but rather how they can forge a mutually beneficial relationship over time.

Focus on building deep and meaningful connections with your network. Be genuine, compassionate, and interested in their life and experiences. Do not shy away from asking for advice or helping when you can. This builds trust, and as your connections grow and evolve, the shared trust and respect can result in mutual growth.

8.5. Mastering The Follow-up

Impressive first meets and fascinating personal branding are incomplete without a diligent follow-up strategy. Wealthy people understand that relationships fade unless nurtured. Thus, they remember to connect and engage with their network periodically, even if there isn't a pressing business matter to discuss.

Tools like LinkedIn, emails or even a traditional phone call can be used to stay in touch. Share useful articles, congratulate on their achievements, or simply check in to see how they are doing.

8.6. Participating in Community Events

Community participation is another profound technique employed by the rich. By being part of social, cultural, and philanthropic events, they diversify their sphere of influence, gaining access to a broader range of individuals from various areas of life. Apart from the networking perspective, it also enhances personal growth and broadens one's perspective.

At the end of this chapter, remember one thing: networking is not a transactional process. It's a journey of learning, sharing and growing together. The wealthy don't just build connections; they cultivate relationships, understanding that the benefits of doing so extend well beyond financial gains. They invest their time, effort, and sincerity in people, and in doing so, they significantly enrich their ability to understand, navigate, and leverage the world in which they thrive.

Chapter 9. Risky-rich: How the Wealthy Leverage Risk

In the world of business and finance, risk and reward are two sides of the same coin. They are the yin and yang that dictate the rhythm of wealth accumulation. Many believe success to be a result of luck or happenstance, but the reality is that the affluent and successful intentionally embrace risk to enable continuous growth.

9.1. Embracing the Risk Factor

The rich understand that risk is not an enemy but a crucial part of the journey to financial success. While most people tuck their heads down and play it safe, preferring the familiar terrain of their comfort zone, the truly wealthy know that fortune indeed favors the bold.

Risk is often misunderstood. It is not about diving headfirst into the unknown recklessly, but meticulously understanding the nature of the venture, potential loss, and gain, and then taking a calculated leap. This enables the rich to transform risk from a wild, uncontrolled element into a finely-tuned instrument of wealth creation.

Think of some of the most prosperous people in the world – Bill Gates, Warren Buffet, Oprah Winfrey, and Elon Musk. Each of them has taken significant risks along their journey, but only after delving deep into analyzing the potential obstacles and the rewards that lay ahead.

9.2. The Power of Calculated Risks

There is a common misconception that the wealthy are lucky—they merely happened to be in the right place at the right time. While timing can play a role, it's rarely the primary engine of their wealth. The truth lies in one of the less emphasized habits of the wealthy: taking calculated risks.

Wilbur Ross, once a Wall Street tycoon, famously said, "The key to making money is to stay invested." Yet, it is quintessential that staying invested does not mean sitting idle. The wealthy keep reassessing their stakes, re-evaluating their investments, and take further risks based on changing market situations, trends, and potential yields.

Calculated risks are not stabs in the dark or hail mary passes. The wealthy invest their time and resources into understanding the risk landscape—they chart the unfamiliar territories, note possible pitfalls, and study the potential rewards.

9.3. Diversification: The Risk Mitigation Tool

While the wealthy have a knack for taking relatively more significant risks than the average individual, they do not put all their eggs in one basket. Diversification is a strategy used by the rich to leverage risk while simultaneously tempering any potential fallout.

Diversification aids in spreading investments across various financial instruments, sectors, regions, aiming to reduce the risk of a single point of failure. If one venture takes a nosedive, the pain is mitigated by the success of others. This strategy doesn't just protect wealth; it provides multiple avenues of growth and potential windfalls.

Despite diversification, losses are inevitable. But remember, the financially savvy don't fear losses. Instead, they view them as opportunities to learn, adjust strategies, and continuously improve their risk calculus.

9.4. Risk Tolerance: A Personal Choice

In the pursuit of wealth and success, each individual has a different threshold for how much risk they are willing to take. This risk tolerance level is a deeply personal parameter, influenced by factors such as age, financial health, personal beliefs, life circumstances, and ultimate financial goals.

While the rich may seem fearless, they too have their limits. The key is that they align their investment strategies with their risk tolerance level, leading to sound and sustainable financial decisions. They never gamble with everything they have—instead, they only risk what they can afford to lose.

9.5. Risk and Investment: A Love Story

If wealth is a sea, investment is the vessel, and risk, the wind that propels it forward. Investments, be they in stocks, real estate, bonds, startups, or other vehicles, inherently carry a certain degree of risk. The wealthy are well aware and accepting of this fact and understand how to navigate the tempestuous seas of investment risks to reach the shores of prosperity.

However, to leverage risk effectively, one must be well-versed in financial basics. Knowing the difference between various types of investments, the volatility underlying each, their past performance, the market trends, and future potential can make the difference between a profitable risk and a costly mistake. Taking the time to educate themselves on these aspects is a habit firmly embedded in the routine of the wealthy.

In navigating risk, there is no failsafe method or silver bullet.

Successful wealth accumulation is a complex game demanding skill, knowledge, and a nuanced understanding of risk. A rich individual does not merely endure the rigors of this game; they relish it, thrive in it, and extract the maximum potential from each investment venture. They do not merely exist in the world of riches; they shape its reality, leveraging every risk and every opportunity to their advantage. Thus, they are not just wealthy; they are wealthy because they know how to embrace and harness risk as an essential stepping stone on their path to prosperity.

Chapter 10. Time is Money: The Art of Productivity

Standing on the precipice of an empire is a heady sensation, the air buzzing with potential. To plunge headlong into your journey, there's a powerful mantra to absorb - time is money. A popular saying, sure, but understanding and genuinely embodying this wisdom is the first step on your path towards abundant prosperity.

The margins between the wealthy and those who languish grows ever wider, not through the mere accumulation of money, but through the management of time. The most affluent figures in our society are not simply those who worked harder, but those who harnessed the clock, bending the minutes and hours of the day to their will.

But how does one seize time? Is it even a resource we can grasp? Buckle up as we delve into the principles guiding the fine art of productivity.

10.1. Harnessing the Power of Time

Productivity dances on the edge of each moment, waiting to be conjured into reality. Those with profound financial success do not possess more hours in a day, but they do manage their time with sheer vigilance, channeling each second towards accelerating their lucrative ambitions.

The essence of supreme productivity is not merely being busy, but ensuring that every tick of the clock moves us closer to our ultimate objectives. It's a match to be played strategically, with an eye always on the goal.

Mapping out your day, assigning judicious slots to your high-priority tasks while leaving buffer zones for unforeseen circumstances, will lay the ideal groundwork for a productive day. Develop a robust nighttime routine to envision your forthcoming day. Then as dawn breaks, your brain starts to decipher the day's rhythm, priming you for diligent productivity.

In the realm of the prosperous, time management systems are a religion. Adopt one that suits your style; be it a digital platform, a paper planner, or smart apps, use these tools to design a day that doesn't slip through the cracks of idle neurosis.

Syntax such as scheduling and prioritizing day-to-day tasks are imperative:

1. High-Priority: These tasks directly impact your wealth-building strategy.

2. Medium-Priority: Important but not crucial tasks for immediate success.

3. Low-Priority: Tasks that need to be done, but can be scheduled for later without any significant loss.

Use this syntax to carve your day into actionable segments, aligning your actions with the goals you've set.

10.2. The Hourglass of Focus

The sands of focus shift continuously, and mastering the flow is imperative for productivity. The art of unwavering concentration is a secret weapon employed by the wealthiest among us. Their ability to narrow their field of vision onto a single task at a time catapults their productivity forward.

Practicing mindfulness in your day-to-day activities develops your concentration acumen over time. Another technique to consider is the Pomodoro Technique; the process of hyper-focusing on a task for

25 minutes, followed by a five-minute break. This pattern can train your brain to develop laser-sharp focus.

10.3. The Siesta of Success

Working relentlessly, clocking in numerous hours is often seen as the hallmark of success. But the wealthiest understand that burnout is a grave enemy. Relaxation and rejuvenation are strategic tools employed to maintain the productive pace of their lives.

Designate deliberate time for relaxation within your schedule. Use techniques like meditation or a short nap (a power nap) to revitalize and re-center your energies. It's not a sign of redundancy, but a necessary restorative measure for maintaining high productivity.

10.4. The Network of Time

As the saying goes, "Your network is your net worth." The art of leveraging relationships is vital in the realm of prosperity. Ensuring you're surrounded by innovative minds, seasoned veterans, and ambitious newcomers allows you to cross-pollinate ideas and come up with novel solutions to the challenges you face.

Scheduling time to converse, create and collocate with your network shouldn't be seen as a distraction but a necessary boost to your wealth-building arsenal.

Adapting these principles within your life is not an overnight transition. It's a disciplined journey that requires persistence and relentless passion. Dig deep into these habits, infuse them into your daily living, and watch as the sands of time morph into the golden grains of fortune in your wealth-building journey.

Chapter 11. The Philanthropic Phenomenon: Giving Back to Grow More

The seemingly paradoxical truth about wealth, demonstrated from the lifestyles and practices of affluent individuals across centuries and geographies, is the profound connection between giving and growing. Indeed, philanthropy or giving back isn't merely an afterthought or surplus-oriented shift; it's an integral part of the prosperity loop. This chapter will carefully decode this phenomenon, outlining the various modes of giving, its strategic implementation, the subtle personal and professional benefits, inclusive of case studies that perfectly encapsulate the concept in practice.

11.1. Dynamism of Philanthropy

Philanthropy stretches far beyond the simple act of giving away money. In this present age, it embodies a broader narrative that covers the donation of time, skills, expertise, and social influence. The wealthy consistently prioritize value-adding contributions that cater to society's manifold needs. Whether it's Bill Gates focusing on global health issues, Warren Buffet funding educational initiatives, or Elon Musk propelling environmental sustainability – the various arenas of philanthropy are as diverse as the profiles of its patrons.

Strategically, these contributions are often aligned with the benefactors' field of work or direct sectors of interest. This harmony boosts the efficacy of their efforts, additionally paving the way for mutual growth. Ostensibly, their philanthropy aids the recipients, but beneath the surface, it nurtures the givers' personal and professional development.

11.2. Unraveling the Reciprocal Loop: Gain Through Giving

The essence of philanthropy creates a virtuous cycle: as one generously gives, one also grows, thus enabling further giving.

Surely, each individual's philanthropic journey differs, reflecting their ideologies, interests, and resources. However, patterns emerge across these stories: enhanced personal satisfaction, fortified networks, amplified social standing, and eventually, financial growth. The subsequent sections will delve extensively into these indelible gains of giving.

11.3. Personal Satisfaction: Fulfilling the Soul and the Wallet

Wealth is not a mere accumulation of monetary assets; prosperity must also impact mental and spiritual realms. Numerous studies suggest that philanthropic activities trigger a pleasure response in the brain termed the "helper's high," leading to higher levels of happiness and satisfaction. This dopamine hit can motivate benefactors to further contribute to societal welfare, thus adding to the momentum of the virtuous cycle.

Moreover, giving creates a profound sense of purpose, infusing life with a greater meaning beyond the relentless pursuit of wealth. Arguably, this spiritual richness fosters peace of mind and boosts productivity, indirectly impacting financial prosperity.

11.4. Philanthropy's Profound Impact on Network Expansion

As benefactors delve deeper into philanthropy, they inevitably encounter likeminded individuals, leading to network expansion. These interactions provide an opportunity for collaborative projects, knowledge exchange, and partnership deals. Such networks extend not only amongst individuals in a similar financial bracket but also create bridges to diverse demographic segments that they might ordinarily not encounter. This broadened worldview can thereby enable them to identify unique investment opportunities, driving financial growth.

11.5. Parallels Between Social Stature and Financial Success

Regular philanthropy also bolsters one's social stature. The sheer act of giving back to communities creates a positive personal brand, advancing credibility and announcing reliability. Naturally, these traits are attractive to potential investors, fostering deeper trust bonds. Over time, this augmented reputation can yield considerable dividends, leading to diversified and strengthened avenues of wealth creation and expansion.

11.6. Philanthropy as a Financial Strategy: The Case Studies

Ray Dalio, the founder of Bridgewater Associates, has always given deeply to causes he believes in, such as ocean exploration and mental health. Dalio credits his significant philanthropic efforts, in part, for the successes he's enjoyed while building the world's largest hedge fund.

Azim Premji, the tech billionaire, pledged most of his wealth to his philanthropic foundation, which focuses on equitable and quality-focused education in India. This investment has not only bettered education for a countless number of children but has also spurred industry advancements, further increasing Premji's investments.

11.7. The Long-lasting Impact on Personal and Community Wealth

The philanthropic voyage is not simply about wealth distribution but the creation of wealthier societies. The strategic allocation of resources into areas, such as education, health, and environmental welfare, can cultivate more productive societies. This increased productivity can ultimately lead to wider economic advantages, boosting total wealth for the society and the philanthropist.

In conclusion, philanthropy has evolved far beyond its traditional concept of 'charity.' Today, it's a strategic tool used by the wealthy knowingly or unknowingly to improve personal emotional well-being, expand networks, and enhance social and financial status. The adage, "the more you give, the more you receive," is thoroughly exemplified in the intriguing world of wealth and its accumulation. Philanthropy is undoubtedly a wealth-enhancing habit that ought to be harnessed by those on the path to financial success and resilience.